POEMS IN PRAISE OF
PRACTICALLY NOTIIING

POEMS IN PRAISE OF

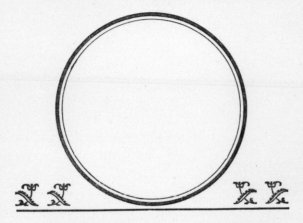

PRACTICALLY NOTHING

SAMUEL HOFFENSTEIN

HORACE LIVERIGHT : *NEW YORK*

Printed in the United States of America

To

EDITH MORGAN

SINCE, AS THEY SAY, THE RARE EXCEPTIONS PROVE
THE RULE IN LIFE AND LETTERS, EVEN LOVE,
THE RULE OF MY DISPRAISES SEEMS MORE TRUE
BECAUSE OF THAT MOST RARE EXCEPTION, YOU.

Some of the verses in this book were first printed in *The New York World, The New York Tribune, Vanity Fair, The D. A. C. News,* and *Snappy Stories.*

Contents

	PAGE
PROEM	11
SONGS TO BREAK THE TEDIUM OF RIDING A BICYCLE, SEEING ONE'S FRIENDS, OR HEARTBREAK	15
VERSES DEMONSTRATING THAT NO MAN CAN BE UNHAPPY AMID THE INFINITE VARIETY OF THIS WORLD, AND GIVING THE READER CHOICE OF SEVERAL TITLES, THE AUTHOR'S FAVORITE BEING, "SOME PLAY GOLF AND SOME DO NOT"	21
POEMS OF PASSION CAREFULLY RESTRAINED SO AS TO OFFEND NOBODY	29
PSALM	41
POEMS INTENDED TO INCITE THE UTMOST DEPRESSION	47
POEMS IN PRAISE OF PRACTICALLY NOTHING	53
NOTES FOR A SUPERFLUOUS POEM	65
A GARDEN OF VERSES FOR THE LITTLE ONES, INCLUDING ORPHANS AND STEP-CHILDREN, AND THEIR PARENTS AND GUARDIANS ALSO	69

PAGE

PANACEA 85

SONGS ABOUT LIFE AND BRIGHTER THINGS YET;
A SURVEY OF THE ENTIRE EARTHLY PANORAMA,
ANIMAL, VEGETABLE, AND MINERAL, WITH AP-
PROPRIATE COMMENT BY THE AUTHOR, OF A
PHILOSOPHIC, WHIMSICAL, HUMOROUS, OR PO-
ETIC NATURE—A TRULY REMARKABLE UNDER-
TAKING 89

SONGS FOR AN OLD-FASHIONED LUTE 115

LITANY BEFORE ELECTION 127

THE MIMIC MUSE 131

SONGS OF FAITH IN THE YEAR AFTER NEXT . . 157

ANTHROPOLOGICAL NOTE 167

INTERLUDE, FOR A SOLITARY FLUTE 173

SONGS OF FAIRLY UTTER DESPAIR 189

CAROL FOR THE DAY AFTER CHRISTMAS . . . 201

LOVE SONGS, AT ONCE TENDER AND INFORMATIVE
—AN UNUSUAL COMBINATION IN VERSES OF THIS
CHARACTER 205

EPILOGUE 217

PROEM

Proem

How exquisite my sorrows look
Neatly marshalled in a book,
Hung on the iambic line
In an orderly design!

See how smooth my trouble goes!—
Printer, weep not on my woes,
Lest your sympathetic grief
Make a blot upon the leaf!

Sweetheart, sigh not for the drear
Winter of my spirit's year,
Lest it vanish—and I can't
Manage the trochaic chant!

Let the winds of fortune blow
To the metres that I know:
There are always better times
Waiting to corrupt our rhymes.

SONGS TO BREAK THE TEDIUM OF RIDING A BICYCLE, SEEING ONE'S FRIENDS, OR HEARTBREAK

Songs to Break the Tedium of Riding a Bicycle, Seeing One's Friends, or Heartbreak

I

Along the country roads there grow
Willow-trees and Texaco,
Mobiloils and marigold
And other fruits of men and mould.
Oh, how my town-tried heart desires
To know the peace of Kelly Tires,
To hear the robin in the grass
Sing, "Socony," as I pass!
Some day I shall fly the rut
And build a small, bucolic hut,
Trim a hedge and hop a stile,
Walk my Camel for a mile,
Milk a mid-Victorian cow—
Eventually, but not now.

II

My luck with the proverbial sex
Should rile, torment me and perplex;
Should turn my simple psyche sour
As, *par exemple*, Schopenhauer.
It should imbue me with disgust
Of woman's misproportioned dust;
Should make me look, with dubious eye,
On every female passerby:
Suspect the sting, mistrust the buzz—
Well, my lad, it does, it does!

III

When trouble drives me into rhyme,
Which is two-thirds of all the time,
What peace a thought like this can give—
Great is the age in which we live!
My heart is heavy, but I know
They're working on the radio;
That letters, by aerial post,
Go every day from coast to coast.
I may be sunk beyond repair,
Drunk less on liquor than despair,
And yet my heart leaps up when I
Behold *Sweet Caporal* in the sky.
Though winter-bare my solitude,
Though heartbreak in its branches brood,

I know that future wars will be
Fought by super-chemistry,
And, therefore, loneliness and loss
Are but a mask for applesauce;—
For I am lord of life and death,
Who flaunt this flaming shibboleth:—
No matter what the morrow brings,
Inventors are inventing things!

IV

Between the mighty legs of Death
We play the schoolboy pranks of breath;
Scrawl challenge on his sodden boots,
The while he coils his cypress-roots.

V

I do not question Woman's place:
She's entered in the human race;
She has a natural turn of mind
For propagation of her kind;
She is—that is to say, a few—
Fairly decorative too,
And on her once maternal breast—
The vogue is past—men used to rest.

If, in this golden age of dames,
She stalks a few surprising claims,
Attempts to puzzle and perplex
Old Nature with a change of sex,
And tumbles from her ancient shelf
In trying to express herself—
Ah, who am I to bid her stay,
Nor try to shave the Mennen way!
There may be some, whose ways are meek;
Who dream submission to a sheik;
Who'd like to waste their love and care
And sweetness on a desert heir;
Who are not fretting to be free
Of orthodox biology;
(If such there be, go mark one well,
And hold her in some citadel!)
But Woman, as they say in Greece,
Is on the hoof for Bigger Fleece:
Too long a serf, too long oppressed
By butter 'n' egg men from the West,
By whiskered juries, blunt of wit,
Who take two hours to acquit.
I hope she finds her proper niche,
Her why and wherefore, what and which,
For through the town I sadly roam,
And note, her place is not the home.

VERSES DEMONSTRATING THAT NO MAN
CAN BE UNHAPPY AMID THE INFINITE
VARIETY OF THIS WORLD, AND GIVING THE
READER CHOICE OF SEVERAL TITLES, THE
AUTHOR'S FAVORITE BEING, "SOME PLAY
GOLF AND SOME DO NOT"

*Verses Demonstrating That No Man Can Be
Unhappy Amid the Infinite Variety of This
World, and Giving the Reader Choice of
Several Titles, the Author's Favorite Being,
"Some Play Golf and Some Do Not"*

Oh, how various is the scene
Whereon we spend our day!—I mean,
Oh, how various is the scene
Allowed to Man for his demesne!
But let's get on—Hip, hip, hurray-o!
Gloria in excelsis Deo,
Who gave us such variety
That none need discontented be;
That each may find his proper niche:
The poor, the maimed, the wretched rich,
The saint (ha, ha!), the son—I mean,
Oh, how various is the scene!—
The earth, whose aspects countless are
As bugs and sneezes in catarrh;

The changeful world so full of things,
From happy deuces down to kings,
That each, no matter how distressed
May find some thing of in-ta-rest.

Consider first topography,
Climate and geography:
Here's the land and there's the sea;
Here's a hill and there's a valley;
Here's a street and there's an alley;
Here's a mountain capped with snow;
Yon, yes, yon's, a swell plateau;
Here's a forest full of trees;
There's a meadow full of fleas:—
Oh, how various is the scene!
(You know exactly what I mean.)
Here is Paris, there is Rome;
Hither's Newark, thither's Nome;
Here is Kansas, yonder's Cork;
Here is Cairo, there New York;
Here the heathen, slightly bored,
Hymns his freshly-baptized Lord,
There's Detroit and Henry Ford:—
Oh, how various is the scene!—
(You know exactly what I mean.)
Well, here it's cold and there it's hot;
Here it's raining, there it's not;
Here it's north and there it's south;
Yon it's wet, but here, what drouth!

Here the tiger eats raw meat;
There the walrus flaps his feet;
Here it's dark and there it's light;
First comes day, and then comes night;
Here it's solid, yon it's air;
Here it's here, and there it's there:—
Oh, how various is the scene
Allowed to Man for his demesne,
So full of this and that and them,
That living is a perfect gem;
That each, no matter what his lot,
May know it's cold while he is hot;
May rapture find in deepest woe
That there it's high while he is low.

Turn we now the other cheek,
And note how various is the week;
Now it's Thursday, now it's Sunday,
Now it's Friday, now it's Monday—
(Blessed be His lavish ways:
There are even other days!)
Tuesday, Saturday and Friday:—
None is *your* day, none is *my* day;
Each belongs to one and all—
Sick or well or great or small:—
Oh, how various is the scene
Whereon we live—well, what I mean
Is—wretched, poor, or blind, or lame,
Sing we praises to His Name!

Now in ecstasy we trace
The aspects of the human race:
Some are men and some are women;
Some—well, anyhow they're human;
Some are short and some are tall;
Some are big and some are small;
Some are dark and some are fair;
Some are bald and some have hair;
Some have all their teeth, but most
To dentists go and eat milk toast:—
Oh, how various is the scene!—
(You know exactly what I mean.)
Well, some are lean and some are fat;
Some are this and some are that;
Some eat kidneys, some eat frogs;
Some keep horses, some keep dogs;
Some are colored, some are white;
Half are sober, half are tight;
Some wear tweed and some wear serge;
Most have some peculiar urge;
Some have money, some have hives;
Some have hope and some have wives;
Some to crime for profit go;
Some hold office, high and low;
Some have gravel, some have gout;
Some like home, but most go out;
Some are cold and some are hot;
Some play golf and some do not!

Oh, how various is the scene
Allowed to Man for his demesne,
That each, no matter what his blows,
May find a poultice for his woes;
May drive his pains and bills away
With tiger, walrus, night or day;
With north or south or west or east,
Or various kinds of bug and beast;
With Latvia or Rumania,
Greece or Pennsylvania,
Newark, Paris, Akron, Cork,
Cairo, Oslo or New York;
With Tuesday, Wednesday, Friday, Sunday,
Thursday, Saturday or Monday;
With tall or short, or stern or slack,
Or those who like their coffee black;
With those in tweed, or those in serge;
With those who dare, or on the verge;
With cold or hot or fat or lean—
Oh, how various is the scene!—
So full of so and so and so,
That none, come weal or woe, woe, woe,
Amid such swell variety
Can ever discontented be.

POEMS OF PASSION CAREFULLY RESTRAINED
SO AS TO OFFEND NOBODY

Poems of Passion Carefully Restrained So as to Offend Nobody

I

You have a most attractive pan,
And I'm a very foolish man,
And, what between the two, I fell
As deep as Dante into hell;
But do you, in your triumph, think
I'll stay forever on the blink,
And pine and pale and waste away
And grow cadaverous and gray—
A wreck, a rum, a shard? Well, maybe
You are right about it, baby!

II

When you're away, I'm restless, lonely,
Wretched, bored, dejected; only
Here's the rub, my darling dear,
I feel the same when you are here.

III

Psycho-analyzed, I stand
And meditate your little hand;
Your lost, evasive eyes, that seem
To lean upon me while they scheme;
And thus contemplative, I know
Why I adore and need you so:—
When I was six or seven or eight,
In that divine, pre-nubile state,
I had a horror, vent in yelpings,
Of what were known as single helpings;
When I was nine, or maybe ten,
I nursed an unrequited yen:
I loved her, middle-aged and shrewish,
That she was Gentile, I but Jewish—
Though now I marvel at it all,
Who am devout Episcopal—
When I was in my 'teens, I dreamed
Green apples were not what they seemed,
But beasts, inimical to rest,
Who sat upon a fellow's chest;

When I achieved the peak of twenty,
Bad breaks with dames I had aplenty,
Who left my burning love behind,
And each, a complex in my mind;—
Now, to these inhibitions true,
I am a-Freud of losing you,
And, though I fully understand,
I meditate your little hand,
Your eyes that lie as like as not,
And love you, whom I ought to swat.

IV

Lovely lady, who does so
All my waking haunt,
Tell me, tell me, do you know
What the hell you want?

Lady, to whose feet I'd bring
The world, if I could win it,
Are you sure of anything
For a single minute?

You whose eyes can kindle flame
Only Death could smother,
Tell me, please, does any dame
Differ from another?

Was the apple applesauce
Eve ate in the garden?
Aren't you all a total loss?
No? I beg your pardon!

V

Oh, the first kiss is sweet—
Like a bud, like a wafer;
But the last, I repeat,
But the last kiss is safer.

The first kiss is sweet
With an innocent savor;
But the last is like meat
With some salt for its flavor.

Oh, with wonder I look—
You so fair, so capricious!
Say, whose goose did you cook
For a meat so delicious?

VI

Come, my sweet (or what you will)
Let us drink our blasé fill;
Let us give the night and day
To love and neurasthen-i-ay.

Let our nerves and passions rage
In the manner of the age,
Dancing through erotic scenes
To the jazzing endocrines.

You love me and I love you
And a dozen others too;
Let's exchange, with linkèd hopes,
Our amorous kaleidoscopes.

While the Fords the land obscure,
And radio makes the silence poor,
Let us be exhibit Z
In the new pathology.

VII

Belovèd, let our love be quite
Intense and splendid, but polite,
That in the hour of parting, we
May end the matter pleasantly.

Since the foredoomed farewell is core
Of all the mortal evermore,
Let us not mar with present fret
The gracious sequel of regret.

Rather, my little love, let me
Your guide for future lovers be,
Whose pleasure now is sometimes fraught
With envy of the men who taught.

[33]

VIII

I cannot elude you, I cannot escape:
You haunt me in every conceivable shape;—
You're morning and midnight and twilight
    and noon,
Orion, the Dipper, the Lion, the moon.

You keep me enchanted, exalted and true
In snares of the fair and ubiquitous you;
I don't mind your being the glories above—
But here you intrude on the ladies I love!

IX

I wish my mind would let me take
You as you are for your own sake;
A trifle less I might adore,
But then, I should enjoy you more.

But Imagination will
Change and transfigure you, until
I never see you, but it seems
Some glory of you stayed in dreams.

Sometimes I think the only thing
That can the lasting rapture bring,
Is not to see you, but to stay
In love with you and far away.

This is the kind of distant bliss
That Dante got from Beatrice:
A woman singing in the trees
A name, an epic, to the breeze.

And men and women all will prove
This cruel arson against Love—
That he burns all else away
In the belovèd but the clay.

X

Sweetling, try not to forget,
Lest in trying, you remember,
She who blows too hard may get
Flame from the deceptive ember.

Let the attic of your mind
Keep whatever stores are in it;
Do not look too much behind,
Lest you tread the present minute.

I shall pluck the moments now—
Only folly weeps to miss one;
Let some later lover's brow
Wrinkle at the thought of this one!

XI

The rain that falls upon my heart
And on my eyes so wistfully,
Will fall again; I shall not start,
For it will drop so restfully

On eyes that will be pools of quiet,
Upon a heart that will not stir
At memories of ancient riot
Within the rain's sad dulcimer.

Even as it falls upon the ground,
Nor makes the tiniest pebble start,
The rain will fall, nor make a sound
Of anything within my heart—

Neither of the bitter nor the sweet
Of loving you, my dear, my dear—
Though all our moments it repeat,
I, who have loved you, shall not hear.

I shall but stare upon my heaven
Of silent earth and starless stone,
Beyond which, grazing sheep at even
Find peace no greater than my own.

And I, who love you now, my dear,
So wildly that my heart is spent,
Think of the time I shall not hear
Your voice in rain, and am content.

XII

I shall sing a song to you,—
Fair a song as any;
Perfect as a drop of dew—
Rare among the many.

Eager, dancing words will do
Their melodious duty;
Make a lucent mirror, true
To your shining beauty.

I shall coin your golden hair
For a stanza's treasure;
Tame your wild and wayward air
To my love-sick measure.

I shall lift my song and sing
With the voice of doom
The utter loneliness you bring
Into this little room.

PSALM

Psalm

High in His holy spires sits the Lord;
He is the bell, the clapper and the cord,
And, taller than the haughty traffic towers,
He sprinkles chimes on the congested hours;
Yet near in lovingkindness to the ground,
He breaks the Sabbath—with His fruitful sound.

Benign and Undenominational,
His benisons from myriad belfries fall:
No special steeples His affections hold,
And styles of architecture leave Him cold;
The stately Gothic in the city fogs,
The shingle Baptist in the rural bogs,
The tricky Moorish, surly Muscovite,
Are equally His dwellings and delight.

With sweet democracy, He plays upon
The simple bell, orchestral carillon,

That he who runs may listen, if not read,
To clangor suited to his secret need,
And know, in toil or wedlock, woe or fear,
That God is ever present in his ear.

He is the bell, the clapper and the cord;
The sacerdotal brokers on the board;
The cost of maintenance, the preacher's hire,
The congregation and agnostic choir;
He is, in short, the works, the church entire,
Electing thus, in stone and wood to stand,
That we His love might readily command,
Who else had power, amid divine acclaim,
To call each cherub by her Christian name.

Oh, mighty abnegation, how you shame
My simple sorrows even out of name!
Who but the Lord such sacrifice could make—
To dwell in bishops for his brother's sake?
Who else desert the lovely seraphim,
To be a hallelujah and a hymn,
Or stand, for thankless mankind, year on year,
High Church in London, neo-Jewish here?

Ring out, ring out, ye non-sectarian chimes!
Inspire these pseudo-democratic times!
From Coast to Coast (or even further) roll
Your living Esperanto of the soul!—
The Methodist, anticipating hell,
Is saved from madness by a Baptist bell;

A complex caught in a Semitic brain
A Presbyterian clapper cures again;
And many a Christian Scientist's despair,
When acidosis was still new to prayer,
Was exorcised by brave St. Patrick's peal,
The uric acid flying at its heel,
Because the rival belfry had the grace
Of therapy in his peculiar case.

Oh Lord, I cannot praise too loftily
Your distribution of Divinity;
Ubiquitous, accessible and free,
Benevolent, beneficent and wise;
Each church, Yourself, and of Yourself a guise,
Yourself in all, and yet all different,
To suit the varied need and temperament;—
Sweet stations set along the path of strife,
The via dolorosa of this life.
The melancholy of insolvent days
The Synagogue Emanu-el allays;
And bright St. Thomas, flawless as a rose,
Is my specific for domestic woes;
St. John, that lifts a hummock to a hill,
Whose dome the Lord expands Himself to fill,
Distinctively and obviously divine,
Protects my teeth above the danger line.
And so the blessed catalogue goes on
Through brick and stone and bell and carillon;
The mystic and eternal ministry
That suits each need and each calamity.

High in His holy spires sits the Lord;
He is the bell, the clapper and the cord;
The seventy-thousand aches and pains and needs;
The twenty-thousand therapeutic creeds;
The church, the book, the candles and the chimes;
The Author of my reason and these rhymes.

POEMS INTENDED TO INCITE THE UTMOST DEPRESSION

Poems Intended to Incite the Utmost Depression

I

When love, at last, had left me quiet,
And my heart was clear of pain,
Toxins, due to faulty diet,
Broke it right in two again.

Those who forge our fates above,
Little heed the hurt they do—
Now with toxins, now with love,
They break our trusting hearts in two.

II

Cervantes, Dostoievsky, Poe,
Drained the dregs and lees of woe;
Gogol, Beethoven and Keats
Got but meager share of sweets;

Milton, Homer, Dante, had
Reason to be more than sad;
Cæsar and Napoleon
Saw the blood upon their sun;
Martyr, hermit, saint and priest
Lingered long at Sorrow's feast:
Paid with pyre and perishing
For every feather in each wing;—
Well, if such as these could be
So foredoomed to misery,
And Fate despise her own elect—
What the deuce do *you* expect?

III

You have dreamed, enduring sorrow,
Of a time yclept tomorrow,
When, your share of trouble spent,
You would flower in content,
Trust your woman, sleep till noon,
Keep your teeth and grab the moon:—
Well, tomorrows came your way
And behaved just like today;
Came in droves and caravans
And thumbed their bugles at your plans.
Yet you have the nerve to say,
"Tomorrow is another day,"
And stake your heart upon a boon
From some tomorrow, surnamed Soon.

Incorrigible boob, I hate
Like poison to vaticinate,
But you, who'll never learn a thing,
Listen to the song I sing:
Ere the last tomorrow's gone,
You'll slice moons in Matteawan.

IV

In a million years or so,
Maybe yes and maybe no,
Maybe sooner, like as not,
Sun and stars will go to pot.
They will leave behind no spark:
Earth will curdle in the dark;
Men like women will become,
Adding to their dreadful sum;
A. E. Housman will come back
And take an even gloomier tack.
Nothing I could say or think,
Or fancy, or project in ink,
Would even by one-tenth convey
The horrors of that monstrous day.
And 'tis for this you toil and sweat;
And 'tis for this you moil and fret;
And 'tis for this that men must weep
While women work them while they sleep!
Of course, you say, "A lot I care:—
My heart is weak, I won't be there;

When that time comes, I'll be about
As dead as love the third week out."
Blind oaf, enjoy your vain delight:—
They'll resurrect you just for spite;
They'll haul you from your dreamless bed
To drop a comet on your head.
And 'tis for this you toil and sweat
And moil, et cetera, et cet.,
And wonder if some feeble dame
Still loves her zany, just the same.
Oh, greatest ape that ever was,
I hope she does, I hope she does!

POEMS IN PRAISE OF PRACTICALLY
NOTHING

Poems in Praise of Practically Nothing

I

You buy some flowers for your table;
You tend them tenderly as you're able;
You fetch them water from hither and thither—
What thanks do you get for it all? They wither.

II

Only the wholesomest foods you eat;
You lave and you lave from your head to your feet;
The earth is not steadier on its axis
Than you in the matter of prophylaxis;
You go to bed early and early you rise;
You scrub your teeth and you scour your eyes—
What thanks do you get for it all? Nephritis,
Pyorrhea, appendicitis,
Renal calculus and gastritis.

[53]

III

You buy yourself a new suit of clothes;
The care you give it, God only knows;
The material, of course, is the very *best* yet;
You get it pressed and pressed and *pressed* yet;
You keep it free from specks *so* tiny—
What thanks do you get?   The pants get shiny.

IV

You practice every possible virtue;
You hurt not a soul, while others hurtue;
You fetch and carry like a market basket—
What thanks do you get for it?   Me don't ask it!

V

You leap out of bed; you start to get ready;
You dress and you dress till you feel unsteady;
Hours go by, and still you're busy
Putting on clothes, till your brain is dizzy.
Do you flinch?   Do you quit?   Do you go out
      naked?—
The least little button, you don't forsake it.
What thanks do you get?   Well, for all this mess, yet
When night comes around, you've got to undress yet.

VI

You're kind to women, children, worms;
You speak of God in the highest terms;
You help spell words like "tetrahedral";
You show respect for a cathedral;
You're sweet and gentle as a mouse is:
(Wives should behave so to their spouses!)
Though women tempt you, more than plenty,
Your rate is half a girl in twenty;—
In short, from grace you never fell yet—
And what do you get? On all sides hell yet!

VII

Your life's a wreck; you're tired of living,
Of lending, spending, borrowing, giving;
Of doubt and fear, of hope and question,
Of women, children and digestion;
There isn't a single dream you cherish—
You simply pine and pray to perish.
You haven't the nerve to take bichloride,
But you stay up nights till you're gaunt and sore-
        eyed;
You don't eat greens, as the doctors tell you,
And you drink the very worst they sell you;
You've earned, at least, let's say, cirrhosis—
And what do you get for it? Halitosis!

VIII

You take a bath, and sit there bathing
In water cold, in water scathing;
You scrub till you're *sans* an epidermis,
And feel like a regular bathing Hermes.
You do not waste a single minute;
The tub shows how you worked while in it;
You dry, and do some honest rooting
For such remarkable abluting:—
Well, a day goes by, or ten, or thirty,
And what thanks do you get? You're just as dirty!

IX

You meet a girl and you surrender;
Though God knows why, you're kind and tender;
You're husband, lover, sister, brother,
Companion, banker, father, mother;
You try your best to be worthy of her;
You make mistakes, but she knows you love her;
You're hers completely, and you show it:
And what thanks do you get? The gate—I know it!

X

You're a good girl; you're gray with virtue;
The very thought of a misstep hurts you;
You know that honor must be hoarded
Against the day when it is rewarded;

You see a girl who's all men's vassal,
Marry a duke in his own castle;
You see another, who can't say, "No, sir,"
Capture, at least, a wholesale grocer;—
But you never let your thoughts grow sordid:
You know in your heart you'll be rewarded.
Well, the years go by, like queens and roses,
The way they did in the time of Moses,
And what do you get? False teeth, a doorman,
A complex, or assistant foreman!

XI

You hire a cook, but she can't cook yet;
You teach her by candle, bell, and book yet;
You show her, as if she were in her cradle,
Today, the soup, tomorrow, a ladle.
Well, she doesn't learn, so although you need her,
You decide that somebody else should feed her:—
But you're kind by birth; you hate to fire her;
To tell a woman you don't require her—
So you wait and wait, and before you do it,
What thanks do you get? She beats you to it!

XII

You're a pure spirit; you're air and water;
You're nobody's son and nobody's daughter;

In short, you're still in the state pre-natal—
A strange condition, but seldom fatal—
Well, anyhow, you're a harmless atom,
Content to stay in your own stratum;
You do not drink or play the horses,
Or interfere with natural forces,
Indulge in moods or whims erratic,
Which cause the flu, and sometimes, static:—
A perfect type of the homo *non est*,
You're unobtrusive, kind and honest,
As upright as an ear of corn—
And what thanks do you get for it all?   You're
    born!

XIII

You're a positive fiend for life extension:
You eat greens in every dimension;
You know as well as any parrot
The quirks of calory and carrot—
They've taken out, without a quiver,
Your tonsils, teeth, ambition, liver,
Appendix, income—every center
Designed to let bacilli enter.
You never miss the daily dozen
That killed your uncle, brother, cousin;
You breathe only the freshest breezes—
And what do you get? The same diseases.

XIV

You work and work, and keep on working,
While poets, even worse, are shirking;
Your hair falls out, your eyes grow bleary,
Your bones grow old, your outlook dreary;
But you never seek to break the fetters—
You go on filing useless letters.
Well, a day arrives, and it must be spring yet;
The birds, somehow, begin to sing yet;
The grass is green, the cows are mooing,
The flies are buzzing, the people shooing,
The air is fresh—it makes you tipsy—
And, all of a sudden, you turn gipsy.
So you come in late, you go home early;
The thought of the office makes you surly;
You come in later, you go home earlier;
The thought of the office makes you surlier;
You've worked enough; you've earned the leisure
To have some poor, but honest pleasure;
No desk, you think, should rise and quell you—
And what do you get?   Do I have to tell you?

XV

You go to high school, even college;
You become a regular Book of Knowledge;
You learn that Nero played the fiddle;
That the Sphinx is, after all, a riddle;

That women weep while men go faring;
That Bismarck seldom was a herring.
No matter what a person asks you,
The brilliant answer never tasks you;
You smile and say, "Go ask another,"
Like, "Did the Gracchi have a mother?"
Well, you meet a girl, and nothing sweeter;
The kind—well, anyhow, you meet 'er—
You look her over with elation—
She seems to have a cerebration:
So you start right in, like Kipling's thunder,
To be the twenty-seventh wonder;
You spout such high and fancy learning,
You're sure the girl will die of yearning—
And when you're finished, did you please her?
Did you hear her say, "You're Julius Cæsar"?
What thanks did you get? The usual solo:
She likes the Prince of Wales and polo.

XVI

You're born (whose fault is it?) a poet—
Nobody sees it, but you know it;
You try to temper your psychoses
And get, at least, Grade B neuroses;
But it's no use—so great the curse is,
You go from bad to worse, then verses.
But suppose you wrote a poem a minute,
What menace, after all, is in it?

You might have been a chiropractor,
Dentist, diplomat, or actor,
Banker, lawyer, politician,
Or, let us say, your own physician,
Attacked the world, and brought upon it
More harm than even a first-rate sonnet—
Here is your chance, but you eschew it;
You haven't quite the heart to do it—
And what thanks do you get for it? Don't I know
    it?—
You go on being a sap and poet.

NOTES FOR A SUPERFLUOUS POEM

Notes for a Superfluous Poem

We chose with care and dined with zest,
A simple fare by genius dressed,
Then home by glittering stars we walked,
And looked on heaven, and gaily talked,
And dreamed a morrow fair as fair,
And drank the bootleg autumn air.
We loved the town for all its bright
Adornment of the naked night,
Its orchid rarities of light.
We loved the town and all its horde,
Whom God has socked but never floored,
And (woe to us!) we loved the Lord.

Then home, and while the night relaxed,
And noises waned, and silence waxed,
We scored against our foes above
That brief perfection which is love.

We took the autumn in and made
A fire for him, and thoughtful shade,
And comfortable at his knees,
We listened to his odysseys,
Until he dropped his misty head,
Was silent. Then we went to bed.

Ah, sequel terrible to tell!
Ah, dreadful sequel that befell!—
Scarce had I tasted slumber's cup,
And scarce prepared on dreams to sup—
An awful nightmare ripped me up!
A nightmare fit for Sisyphus
Leaped up from sizzling Tartarus
And seized me in his brutish paws,
And bit me with his Stygian jaws,
And made a shard, a shred, a patch,
A rag, a wreck, a weed, a thatch,
A heap of dust, a scrap, a bit,
Of all the joys preceding it.

Ah, foe (I quote Millay) and friend,
The moral of this tale attend—
No matter what the Lord may send,
Nightmare gets us in the end.

A GARDEN OF VERSES FOR THE LITTLE
ONES, INCLUDING ORPHANS AND STEP-
CHILDREN, AND THEIR PARENTS AND
GUARDIANS ALSO

*A Garden of Verses for the Little Ones,
Including Orphans and Step-children, and
Their Parents and Guardians Also*

I

Primer

The camel has a funny hump—
  Well, what of it?
The desert is an awful dump—
  Well, what of it?
The sun it rises every day—
  What about it?
Roosters crow and asses bray—
  What about it?
The stars shine nearly every night—
  Don't bother me with it!
Grass is green and snow is white—
  Get out o' here!

II

Yes, Dear

God gave us the blue sky above,
　　And I'll forgive Him that.
He made your mother, marriage, love,
　　And I'll forgive Him that.
God made the grass, the trees, the dew,
　　And I'll forgive Him that.
He also made such boobs as you,
　　And that's where He loses out with me!

III

Lullaby

Yes, I'll take you to the zoo
　　To see the yak, the bear, the gnu,
And that's the place where I'll leave you—
　　Sleep, little baby!

You'll see the lion in a rage,
The rhino, none the worse for age;
You'll see the inside of a cage,—
　　Sleep, little baby!

IV

The Pansy

The pansy makes such weird grimaces,
And imitates all bestial faces—
But there's a thing it couldn't do,
And that is, make a face like you.
I'm sure I've never seen another,
And that you got it from your mother.

V

Lullaby

Hush, my darling, that infernal
Racket; dearest, do!
Mamma is not all maternal—
She's a woman too.
Papa may of mamma tire;
  He's been wed too long;
But the others who admire
Cannot all be wrong.
  Sleep! Sleep!

Men must work, and so they should, dear,
Lest their women weep;
Drawing water, hewing wood, dear,
Helps them go to sleep.

But your mamma sleeps in daytime,
When the sparrows twit,
And when night is here, her playtime,
Mamma wants to flit.
   Sleep! Sleep!

Now I hear the jazzu calling,
Calling to its own—
And if you don't stop your bawling,
You will bawl alone.
Yes, my lambkin, I adore you;
Mamma's kind and true;
But never think because I bore you,
You can bore me too!
   Sleep! Sleep!

VI

The Tree

See the leaves upon the tree!
That is where they ought to be:
Whether they be foul or fair,
Papa did not put them there.

VII

The Doll

Here is the little doll I brought you—
It shows the kind of simp I thought you!

VIII

The Bird

I love to hear the little bird
Into song by morning stirred,
Provided that he doesn't sing
Before my own awakening.
A bird that wakes a fellow up,
Should have been a buttercup.

IX

A Father's Heart is Touched

When I think of all you've got
Coming to you, little tot:
The disappointments and diseases,
The rosebud hopes that blow to cheeses,
The pains, the aches, the blows, the kicks,
The jobs, the women, and the bricks,
I'm almost glad to see you such
An idiot, they won't hurt you much.

X

Lullaby

Sleep, my little baby, sleep;
You'll have cause enough to weep—
Slumber is a precious boon;
You'll be getting measles soon;

Mumps will claim you for their own;
Croup will change your infant tone.
Sleep, my little darling, sleep,
Ere your first bicuspids peep
Through your rosy little gums,
And the envious colic comes.
Oh, the troubles Time will ladle
On your happy baby cradle
Very shortly from the deep!—
So, be wise, my lamb, and sleep.

XI

Zoology

The elephant's a ghastly beast
That haunts the countries of the East;
The hippopotamus, I think,
Never gets enough to drink;
At any rate, I hear the dub
Never leaves his muddy tub;
The eagle dwells upon the steep
And feeds on savages and sheep—
What's the good of having that
Awful rot beneath your hat?

To a Chubby Little Girl, Aged Three

The jungle is a kind of grove
Where lions, apes and rajahs rove;
It's not the kind of place that I
Should choose to live in, or to die;
Yet I should just as soon be in it
As hear you blab another minute.

XIII

The Wind in the Tree

When the wind is in the tree,
It makes a noise just like the sea,
As if there were not noise enough
To bother one, without that stuff.

XIV

The Calf, the Goat, the Little Lamb

The calf, the goat, the little lamb,
How easy is their day!
They do not seem to give-a-damn
For anything but play.

Each hour its simple pleasure brings,
And not a thing to do,
And yet, like other living things,
They end up in a stew!
And so did I, my little lamb,
And so will you.

XV

The Gnu

The gnu is a remarka-bul,
From all descriptions, ani-mul;
Yet how remarka-bul must you
Appear to the eccentric gnu!—
I have no doubt that even I
Must puzzle his peculiar eye;
There's something wrong with all of us;—
Let's ask the hippopotamus.

XVI

Papa Sings (And How!)

The moon is made of Stilton cheese;
Polar bears can never freeze;
In summer there are lots of flies;
Pumpkins end in pumpkin pies;

[76]

Rivers flow into the sea;
You don't look a bit like me;
When it's winter, then it snows,—
Scoot! You've got your mother's nose!
Germans drink a lot of beer—
Now, you pest, get out o' here!

XVII

Mamma Sings

Go to sleep, my little oaf,
Mamma's darling sugar-loaf;
Go to sleep and stay that way
For at least a night and day;
I'm no angel up above—
Don't abuse my mother-love;
I can stand so much and then
Mamma wants maturer men.
Sleep, my little plague, sleep tight;
My complexes are bad tonight,
And papa's friend is waiting now
To add a horn to papa's brow—
So sleep, my onus, sleep my own,
For if you bawl, you bawl alone.

XVIII

For Drum and Harmonica

Sleep, my darling baby, sleep:
The French eat frogs; Australians, sheep.

Today will go, tomorrow come;
I'll bake a cake and give you some.

Angels through your slumber sing!
A kangaroo's a funny thing.

A kangaroo will make you laff,
But not so much as a giraffe—

Not so much as a giraffe;
I'll bake a cake and give you haff—

A chocolate cake and a gooseberry tart;
Sleep, my darling; have a heart!

Don't you worry; ma will keep—
You yelled all day and now you sleep!

XIX

For Little Boys Destined for Big Business

Sleep, my baby, little elf;
Grow up honest—with yourself!
Always unto others do
What they'd like to do to you.

Love your neighbor—he may be
Useful; and besides it's free;

But should he more than friendship seek,
Always turn the other cheek.

Help the needy—all that's lent
Brings from six to ten per cent;
Place your trust in Heaven, but keep
Your money working while you sleep.

Loyal be to loyal friends;
Make them pay you dividends;
Work, like the industrious bee,
Your friends and foes impartially.

While the tender conscience frets,
All things come to him who gets;
All that glitters will for gold
Glitter more a thousand-fold.

Plutocratic precious, sleep:
Finer feelings all will keep;
Easy lies the head that wears
A crown among both bulls and bears.

XX

For Little Boys in General

Hush, my darling; do not cry—
You'll have cause to, by and by;
Blonde or Titian or brunette,
Some of them will get you yet.

[79]

You'll grow up and then you'll fall—
You'll have reason then to bawl;
You'll be glad to get some sleep,
For men must work, or women weep.

Men must work, while women try
To want the things they have to buy,
And while they try so hard to want,
Men must labor and grow gaunt.

When I look at baby's brow,
How I hate the hussies now!
Mamma'd save you if she could—
Sleep now, while the sleeping's good!

XXI

For Little Girls Only

Rock-a-bye, baby; why do you smile?
Are you rehearsing how to beguile?
We'll mould your expression just the right way:
Your natural look is a bit too blasé.

Mamma will tuck her little one in;
Sleep now, my darling, it's good for the skin;
And skin is important, for soon comes the day
When baby commences her skin game to play.

Mamma will help you, mamma advise,
Take the hard look away from your eyes;
Mamma will tell her lamb what to do,
Then Ziegfeld will come and glorify you.

PANACEA

Panacea

I chant the homely bard who sings
The solace of insentient things;
Who lays upon his gall and grief
Balsamic bush and unguent leaf;
Who slips his humors to the hill,
His dolors to the daffodil.
I've taken many a desperate chance
With seventy kinds of shrubs and plants;
Consigned my toothache to the trees,
My heartbreak to the Pleiades.
The red and therapeutic rose
Has healed me of corrosive woes,
And much I owe of health and ease
To blooming beets and peonies.
When trouble smote me, zip and thigh,
I've winked at the narcotic sky;
I've taken creditors to stare
Upon the liquidating air,

And soothed the bloodhounds in their breast
With, "See the sun sink in the West!"
I've clipped misfortune's panther paw
With natural phenomena,
And poulticed worry and disease
With Christian Science cabbages.
Oh, let the years their sorrows yield—
The brook is gurgling through the field;
The high and homœopathic stars
Will heal my wounds and leave no scars;
The rainbow hurdle miles and miles
Of zooming Fords and cloudy stiles,
To lay upon my fear and fret
Her cool and glowing amulet,
While panaceas straight from God
Leap up in lilies from the sod.

Oh, hail, the homely bard who sings
The solace of insentient things:
The sky, the sea, the air, the ground,
Where perfect lenitives abound!

SONGS ABOUT LIFE AND BRIGHTER THINGS
YET; A SURVEY OF THE ENTIRE EARTHLY
PANORAMA, ANIMAL, VEGETABLE AND MIN-
ERAL, WITH APPROPRIATE COMMENT BY
THE AUTHOR, OF A PHILOSOPHIC, WHIMSI-
CAL, HUMOROUS OR POETIC NATURE—A
TRULY REMARKABLE UNDERTAKING

Songs About Life and Brighter Things Yet;
A Survey of the Entire Earthly Panorama,
Animal, Vegetable and Mineral, with Appro-
priate Comment by the Author, of a Philo-
sophic, Whimsical, Humorous or Poetic
Nature—a Truly Remarkable Undertaking

I

Nothing from a straight line swerves
So sharply as a woman's curves,
And, having swerved, no might or main
Can ever put her straight again.

II

Men in single state should tarry;
While women, I suggest, should marry.

III

Some folks I know are always worried,
That when they die, they will be buried;
And some I know are quite elated
Because they're going to be cremated.

IV

Oh, it is cruel and inhuman
Not to pick up a fallen woman!—
The man who will not pick her up,
Shall have but water in his cup.

V

Where primal instincts do not slumber,
One sex the other does outnumber:
Men, e.g., are scarce in Paris—
The cause of which, *on dit*, the war is—
And the status that prevails
In London is a dearth of males;
While twenty fellows in Manhattan
Jump for the chair that Jenny sat in.
'Tis bad, I think to have too many
Women around a man—if any.

VI

A queen as torrid as Sumatra
Was the famous Cleopatra,
While Queen Elizabeth, I gather,
Contained herself in hottest weather:—
Proving that even queens can vary,
(And how!) like simple Madge or Mary;—
Yet spell them with an a or e,
They look a lot alike to me.

VII

It must be terrible to be
The kind of man they call a "he";
A man who'd rather fight than eat,
And doesn't have to cook his meat;
To whom a million women cling;
Who's not afraid of anything;
Who aims with an unerring eye
When circumstances justify;
Whose breadth and brawn and strength
    and size
Demand continual exercise;
Who rises every day at five
And feels it's good to be alive;
Who burns up leagues of windy plains
While weaklings wilt in subway trains.

Personally, I prefer
To be a guy who hates to stir;
Who stares with moist, suspicious brow
For signs of malice in a cow;
Who couldn't climb upon a horse
With pulleys, ladder, threats or force;
Who hasn't brains enough to care
About the foulness of the air,
And doesn't know that oxygen
Is breathed by all red-blooded men
The wide world over, east and west,
And sprouts in hair upon the chest;—
A fish, who lets his vigor lapse,
In dusty towns, where men are saps;
Who every manly art abhors,
And moulders in the Great Indoors.

Although a man like that disgraces
His brothers of the Open Spaces;
Although his chest is bald and flat,
There's something underneath the hat
Of such a man—a kind of demon
That lets him boss ten thousand he-men,
Who gallop grandly o'er the plains
And bring him home their hard-earned gains;
And though he's anything but strong,
He lives as healthy twice as long.

VIII

I'd rather listen to a flute
In Gotham, than a band in Butte.

IX

The serpent has no feet or hands,
Yet makes his way in many lands;
But who would on his belly crawl
In order to avoid a fall?

X

The leopard cannot change his spots:
In short, they're his forget-me-nots.

XI

Sometimes, in the dead of night,
Beyond the tiger-yellow light,
I hear the silence; then I see
It sprawling cat-wise comfortably,
With high back arched against the skies,
And starry languor in its eyes,
Transparent in transparent air,
Yet darkly outlined to my stare.

Then it occurs to me if that
Content and immemorial cat
Moved its ubiquitous, soft paws,
And opened those impalpable jaws
And spoke—what revelation then
Would flash and thunder upon men;
What light apocalyptic would
Shine from the eyes of evil and good;
What speech articulate would fall
From stars in the air's confessional;
What secrets joy and woe would sing,
And the stone mouth of Everything!

Then it occurs to me, as now,
That all that cats can say is *"Meow!"*

XII

Stars reflected in the water
Are jewels enough for Pharaoh's daughter;
But Pharaoh's daughter's dead and gone
While living girls are getting on.

XIII

The oyster never leaves his shell,
And does, therein, exceeding well;

He does not have to sweat and brood
To know the joys of oysterhood;
He deems the treasured pearl a fault,
And takes his world with ample salt.

XIV

From coast to coast the railroads roam,
Yet every inch of rail stays home.

XV

Twinkle, twinkle, little star,
But stay, my darling, where you are;
Into my life if you should fall,
I'd never see you shine at all.

XVI

There's no one that I'd like to be
One half so much as I or me,
And though I sup on meager bran,
I'd change the menu, not the man.

XVII

They say a rolling stone's a loss:
And yet I see no use in moss;
I'd rather gypsy through Cockaigne
Than vegetate a dubious gain.

XVIII

There are strange creatures in the zoo,
Like emu, zebra, auk and gnu,
But stranger creatures have I seen
Riding in a limousine.

XIX

It drinks up all—and yet the sea
Exceeds not its capacity;
Alas, how much a man must fret
To keep himself as strong—and wet!

XX

Blossoms in a May-day breeze
Are like lovely promises;
They delicately seem to say
That every bud will have its day,
Will blossom, ripen and be fruit,
And very often, canned, to boot!

XXI

The church, for all its Heavenly birth,
Can never leave the lowly earth,
While I, of more profane extraction,
May walk myself into a fraction;

May scale the air, the sky explore,
And knock at Heaven's very door;
Which shows that I have more a mind
For Heaven, than any church you'll find,
And that the spire, which Heavenward points,
Is still with Heaven out of joints.

XXII

I do respect that noble man
Who, when he's full of trouble can
Preserve a bright and cheerful mien
As if his life were all serene;
But I prefer the fellow, who
Is lively as a kangaroo
And beams and shouts with pure delight,
When everything is going right.

XXIII

The ostrich lives in foreign lands
And trots along the burning sands,
And when from foes it would escape,
It hides its head—the silly ape!

XXIV

There's nothing sweeter than a bride
If you're not standing by her side;
But if you are, I learned in books,
You'll never see how sweet she looks.

XXV

The rose is so improvident
It never saves a single scent,
Without which fault, you must agree,
The rose would smell like you or me:—
Alas, that vices often are
The virtues of a flower or star,
Which paints the night upon the deep,
While men and swine are fast asleep.

XXVI

There's nothing that I have to say,
You haven't heard a duller day.

XXVII

The camel has a hump, but he
Looks just as curiously at me.

XXVIII

The tailor sews and gets the pip;
The tailor sews while others rip.

XXIX

The parrot does the best he can
To imitate the talk of Man,
But since he has no gift for speech,
The best the bird can do is screech.

XXX

See the serpent in the grass!
Stand aside, there; let him pass!
Oh, how happy he could be
With the smallest leg-acy!

XXXI

The dinosaur and icthyosaur
Are not among the things that are,
Though once the beasts were features;
Ah, sad it is to contemplate
How Nature can eliminate
Unnecessary creatures!

Perhaps she will, at last, extend
The process to another end—
To man, and even woman,
And turn the final hose of Fate
And give the biologic gate
To the obnoxious human!

XXXII

How doth the busy little bee
Improve each shining hour?   Well, how?
The shining hour, it seems to me,
Still wears no honey on its brow,
Nor is, for all that I can see,
Improved by man or beast or bee.

XXXIII

The apple grows so bright and high,
And ends its days in apple pie.

XXXIV

When I was young, my hopes ran high—
My hopes did run, and so could I;
They danced upon the mountain tops
Oblivious of the traffic cops;

They swung, like monkeys in the trees,
From sun and moon and Pleiades;
They frolicked on the farthest wave
And thumbed their noses at the grave;
They thumbed their haughty bugles long
At men and creeds and right and wrong,
And gave the tin-horn days to come
Their only sound of fife and drum:—
Well, now my thyroid youth is done,
I'm very glad my *hopes* had fun!

XXXV

The ant, he lays aside some dough
Against the time of cold and snow;
He doesn't trust a bit to luck,
But gathers his assorted truck:—
If I could live just like the ant
I'd be as thrifty—but I can't.

XXXVI

The monkey chatters in the tree
Without a point, incessantly,
And thence bequeaths to Man his looks,
His conversation and his books.

[101]

XXXVII

The pansy is so slight a flower,
You'd think it could but live an hour—
So fragile is its grace;
And yet the little thing can dare
The lion's countenance to wear
Upon its pretty face.

How often does the meanest thing
Bestrut its fancy like a king
And walk a royal way!
For every wolf in sheep's attire,
A hundred thousand sheep aspire
To stalk the helpless prey.

XXXVIII

Content with things in miniature,
The humblest gold-fish is not poor;
His small aquarium is quite
Sufficient for his small delight;
He does not crave the flowing stream,
Or of the mighty ocean dream,
But with a little weed and gravel
Will simulate extensive travel.
A crystal dungeon cannot fret
Or chafe his spirit—if it's wet;

But he, with aqueous content,
Makes bright his mean environment:—
Glass walls do not a prison make
For fish who find a bowl a lake;
Who can, factitious weed beyond,
Behold the margin of a pond.

XXXIX

The farmer walks behind the plow
Which mops the ground as he his brow;
The sun, it broils the wretched man
Until the loam is not more tan;
The very horses seem to talk
About him, as before they walk,
Treading with ease their crumbly courses
And quite contented to be horses.
I know that I should rather be
A horse or cow or goat than he,
Which feed upon a natural hoard
Nor sweat and strain to keep a Ford.
A horse is placid, strong and clean,
It reads no Farmer's Magazine;
A barren stall, a simple oat
Are more important than its vote.
If I were on that hillside now
And that man's sweat were on my brow,

XLIII

The miner wears a hob-nailed boot;
His clothes and face are black as soot;
He is a most fantastic sight
Among the lilacs fresh and bright

XLIV

A lot of good it does a guy
To know that June is in the sky;
That in the fields the happy kine
On grass and clover amply dine;
That laurel on the mountain grows,
And bees are feeding on the rose.
I am no cow and cannot eat
Grass and clover 'stead of meat;
I couldn't chew a rose if I
Were threatened by the Wrath on High.
There's nothing I can get with honey—
I'm not a bee; I need the money,
And this bright office where I earn it,
What rose or laurel wouldn't spurn it?
I must admit, a blessed boon
To me is this same month of June.

XLV

I have only a bicycle,
And you have a motor car;
But your wife's a regular icicle
And as blue as the bluest star.

I have only a room and a bath
And you have a swell chateau;
But you're a case for a psychopath
And an allopath or so.

I have only one suit, in sooth,
And you have a couple of score;
But you have only a part of a tooth
Where a whole tooth grew before.

I have little of skittles and gin
And you have scuttles of wine;
But your troubles from women to insulin
Are nothing compared to mine.

XLVI

Tomorrow comes, tomorrow goes;
The thorn intrudes upon the rose;
The bee improves the shining hour
By robbing the defenseless flower,
Affording Man a Heaven-sent
And holy, natural precedent;

The crickets chirping in the dark;
The glow-worms with their sudden spark;
I like the sturdy hills that rise
In gracious worship of the skies;
The grove, the field, the church-like wood,
The sweet, adventurous solitude.
I like to watch the cattle graze
Silent in the sunny days:
The cows, that waking seem to sleep;
The woolly and untroubled sheep,
So simple and so unaware
They seem to blend into the air.
And yet I should be quite cast down
To see the country come to town.
I like the country best for this;—
Because they put it where it is.

LIII

Of all the birds that sing and fly
Between the housetops and the sky,
The muddy sparrow, mean and small,
I like, by far, the best of all.

His lot approaches human life;
His days are full of fear and strife;
He takes the traffic as it comes,
And pounds the sullen pave for crumbs.

No bird has so unsure a span;
He fights the elements and Man;
And so harassed is all his day,
He has no time to sing or pray.

From tenement to tenement
He flees, too frail to get the rent,
And then, his checkered days to crown,
A checkered taxi runs him down.

Songs for an Old-Fashioned Lute

I

I've certainly learned a lot;
I've clarified many confusions;
I know when it's cold or it's hot,
And facts, as distinct from illusions.

I'm properly cynical, too;
Sophisticate, thoroughly urban;
I know what to say and to do,
And what to keep under the turban.

I've listened to Clara and Jane
In many informative sessions,
And I'll never be troubled again
With trifles like dreams and suppressions.

I've a swanky contempt for the sticks,
From Calgary down to the Isthmus,

I'm opposed to the trend of the time,
To the febrile caprice of the minute;
And—wait till I finish this rhyme—
A hell of a lot there is in it!

III

I yodel a bachelor life;
I sing of the joys of the single;
I scoff at a man with a wife,
And laugh at the thought that they mingle.

I cavort and I dine as I please;
I pay court to the vine and to beauty;
I blow (when I'm flush) like a breeze
From acquisitive cutie to cutie.

I am free of the fear of the wed
(For the female's capricious in temper)
That, at last, the inviolate bed
Will enact the familiar *sic semper*.

I am free in my work and my play,
My speech and my dress and my habits;
There is none *ex cathedra* to say
My brightest remarks are like Babbitt's.

I never have need to compete
With the wiles of a popular mummer,
And, provided I'm fond of the heat,
I can stay in the city all summer.

I never am prey to the thought
That my manner of loving and living
Is less than the bozos who taught
The missus the pleasures of giving.

The whimsies I serve are my own,
Be they politics, peaches or ponies,
With never a critical groan
From a creature of different hormones.

I am absolute lord of my time;
I am master and mate of the minute;
And—wait till I finish this rhyme—
A hell of a lot there is in it!

IV

The benedict's lot I espouse,
And my arteries quiver with pity
For the scholar, the sailor, the souse
Alone in the maw of the city.

Wherever they read or they roam,
Their lore and their liquor are hollow—
The sedative honies of home
Allay not the fevers that follow.

I sit in my cozy retreat
Where all but the doorbell is quiet;
The fender takes care of my feet,
And the *frau* does the same for my diet.

VI

With lilies and languors I'm done;
With lotus and beautiful letters;—
I chant of a place in the sun,
And a horse in the van of go-getters.

I tug (as they say) at the leash;
I sniff at the roses of piffle;
I'm finished for good with hasheesh,
The lute and the lyrical sniffle.

The procreant Charles M. Schwab
I laud, as the ancients the phallus,
Who tickles the ducts of the mob
With pride in the virtuous callous.

My waking is loud with Success;
My sleep is impatient and nervous:
I ride with the mighty *noblesse*,
And distribute the coppers of Service.

I am sick of the sixty Beyonds;
Art bores me with every new mania;
I want to be Something in bonds,
And kind to the Queen of Rumania.

I long to be making the grade
And stand with the Mellons and Morgans;
I want to be Genghis of trade,
And Khan of conservative organs.

I play with the bulls and the bears;
I'm the Bartlett of market quotations;
I am in on the private affairs
Of the principal borrowing nations

I am quite *en rapport* with the *Times;*
I am thoroughly up to the minute;
And—now that I'm done with these rhymes—
A hell of a lot there is in it!

Litany Before Election

Oh, Lord, Who knowest the human heart,
(A thousand other things apart)
Whose constant purpose is the good
Of all the human brotherhood—
Look down (accept this humble rhyme)
And guard us in election-time!
Oh, let the people vote for Biggs,
And not for Jiggs, or Squiggs, or Riggs,
Or Kelly, Cohen, Bing or Brown,
Or Toohey, Thompson, Tubbs or Towne!
When sorrow has no more surprise,
And stars look down like Borgia's eyes;
When hope and hair and teeth are gone,
And trucks and I awake the dawn,
How good, in this abyss of care
To know that Biggs is in the chair!
We do so much, perforce, by rote,
And often know not how we vote;
We stumble through the dark below,
But Thou canst see what way we go—

The Mimic Muse

I

The Shropshire Lad's Cousin

(An Even Gloomier Fellow Than His Celebrated Relative)

1

When I was one and twenty,
My ills were in their prime,
With aches and pains aplenty,
And gout before my time;
I had the pyorrhea,
And fever turned me blue—
They said that I would be a
Dead man at twenty-two.

Now I am two and twenty,
The aches and pains I thought
Were miseries aplenty,
Compared to these, are naught;

[131]

They stood beneath the tent-cloth,
And heard the lion roar;
They saw the striped hyena
Revolve upon the floor;
And now they are no more.

I think of all the corpses
Worm-eaten in the shade;
I cannot chew my peanuts
Or drink my lemonade:
Good God, I am afraid!

I see the grave-worms feeding
Upon the tigers' tails;
I see the people quiet
As prisoners in jails,
Because they're dead as nails.

Then what's the good of watching
The horses and trapeze,
The big show and the little,
And the menageries?—
We're all a lot of fleas.

6

I had three friends in Gotham,
And one of them is dead,
And one of them has palsy
And cannot leave his bed.

And now I know the other
Will soon desert me too,
And end his days in Sing Sing,
For something he will do.

7

Northward wing the happy swallows
To their olden haunts again,
And the poison ivy follows,
And the quinsy and the rain.

Soon the lovers will be walking
In the raw, malicious air,
Through catarrhal noses talking
Slush no mortal man can bear.

8

"Terence, this is fearful rot,
Putting poison in the pot;
All your song is measles, mumps,
Cramps and colic and the dumps;
Terence, you are rather frayed—
Go and have your teeth X-rayed."

Go ahead, my lad, and talk,
While your legs are fit to walk;
While your hair is on your head:
You'll not talk when you are dead.

Tied up Cohen and Shultz and Harrigan,
From Portland, Maine, to Portland, Oregon—
Tied them up in knots of air—
Hey, you, Marconi, are you there?
Bill Marconi,
Son of Italy,
Say, you, Marconi, are you there?
I'll say you're there!
There,
There,
There!
Crashing through the air
Without any wire;
I'll say you're there
Like a prairie fire;
Radio,
Radio,
Radio,
Radio!
Right through space with a crash like Zbysco,
From Salem, Mass., to San Francisco!
Hey, there, Buffalo,
Get that soprano!
Hey, there, Idaho,
Get that piano!
Get Paderewski pounding the piano!

X Y Z
W J G
P Q D

Hey, Pennsylvania,
Do you know
That California
Had an inch of snow?
Oklahoma is cloudy and cool,
And they're putting on their rubbers
When they send their kids to school.
Did you hear about the drop
In Minnesota,
And the bumper crop
In South Dakota?—
The bumper, bumper, bumper crop!
Listen in,
You son of sin,
Amalgamated Indigo took another flop;
Flop,
Flop,
Flop!
The ships on the ocean
Beat a retreat;
They're scared to death;
They hold their breath;—
There's a commotion down on the Street;
The bulls and the bears, and the bears and the
     bulls,
Tear one another's hair by the hard handfuls;—
The bulls and the bears
Are at one another's throats;
The bulls and the bears
Get one another's goats!

Your teacher will tell you if she knows her biz;
Your father and your mother,
The corner cop,
Your sister and your brother
Will tell you he's a Wop—
Who would have thought that a guy like that
Would have the radio under his hat?
Well, he did;
Sure, he did;—
What does it matter if it's Dago or it's Yid?
Whoever did is the Kandy Kid;—
Yes, he is;
Sure, he is;
What does it matter where he got his phiz?
Radio,
Radio,
Radio,
Radio!
There's a guy who knew his biz!
There's a boy
Who stirred up things;
Who plays a fiddle without any strings;
Who taught us how to fly
Without any wings.
Hats off to you, Bill;
Hats off, boy;
From Pekin, China,
To Peoria, Illinois.
Radio!
Radio!

X Y Z!
Skips over mountains
And scoops up the sea;—
Who would have thought that a guy like that
Had the radio under his hat?

III

Miss Millay Says Something Too

1

I want to drown in good-salt water,
I want my body to bump the pier;
Neptune is calling his wayward daughter,
Crying, "Edna, come over here!"

I hate the town and I hate the people;
I hate the dryness of floor and pave;
The spar of a ship is my tall church-steeple;
My soul is wet as the wettest wave.

I'm seven-eighths salt and I want to roister
Deep in the brine with the submarine;
I speak the speech of the whale and oyster;
I know the ways of the wild sardine.

I'm tired of standing still and staring
Across the sea with my heels in dust:
I want to live like the sober herring,
And die as pickled when die I must.

[143]

Rose of the World, a pot of gold,
Or even half a pot of gold,
And if you were untrue to me then,
Heart, I would take it back again.

V

Mr. Walter de la Mare Makes the Little Ones Dizzy

1

When winking stars at dusk peep through
Pin-holes in the tent of blue,
Nurse puts spectacles on nose
And points them out to Little Lou.

With sad distempers all awry,
She stares with a myopic eye,
And mumbles names of stars and spheres
As they were letters in the sky.

Orion, Great Bear, Dipper—she
Cons them with a cracked "Tee, hee!"
While wretched Little Lou must keep
Nose to the pane unwillingly.

While ants crawl up and down his back,
She ties him to the zodiac,
And feeds him his astronomy
With many a salty pinch or whack.

Hour by hour goes slowly past;
The stars, like measles, fade at last;
Nurse goes upstairs, but Little Lou
Is to the window frozen fast.

2

When the Great Captain Sun goes home
And calls his spearsmen from the dome,
Sheep-bells, cow-bells, goat-bells and ram-bells
Tinkle and jangle in the gloam.

Pastures that were pistachio green,
In the slate dusk can scarce be seen,
And now are empty, where but late
Quick goats, slow cows, dumb sheep have been.

Then elves, that make the barn their house,
And in the bins and mangers browse,
Bob up and down in oats and hay
And bleat like sheep and moo like cows.

3

Speckled with glints of star and moonshine,
The house is dark and still as stone,
And Fido sleeps in the dogwood kennel
With forelegs over his mutton bone.

Two dozen cows, knee-deep in grass,
I saw, and twenty-seven goats,
And heard a hundred sparrows pour
Upon a bank ten thousand notes.

And, though I've seen the golden notes
That rich men pour in city banks,
And know the sparrow's note is "cheep,"
I lifted up my heart in thanks.

VII

Edwin Arlington Robinson Gets at the Root of the Matter

"Well, now," she said, "that we are met again
Upon familiar terms that yet contain
Enough restraint to make it interesting,
I want to ask you in a friendly way
If you knew Peter Perkins?"
                              "And if so,"
I answered, hiding my perplexity,
"You surely mean what I infer you mean,
That Peter Perkins was a man I knew?"

She smiled that wan and wandering smile of hers,
A soft confusion of her clarity,
And with her little finger flicked away
A speck of gold from out her shining hair.

I knew she heard me though I was not sure,
And cracked my knuckles in a casual way.

"We might as well be somber now," she said,
"And start to psycho-analyze this man.
He had a soul a stranger could see through,
And yet he had a trifling way with him,
Opaque transparency. I think the phrase
Has just enough simplicity to be
Complex enough. Don't crack your knuckles, please,
For Peter Perkins did that very thing.
I don't know why, do you?"

                         I turned away;
I sensed the tragedy in all she said,
Yet could not say a word.

                    "I like to think,"
She wandered on, "that Peter Perkins might
Have been an altogether different man,
If God had made him so. But as it was,
He was but Peter Perkins to the town;
His wife was Mrs. Perkins, and his son
Was Peter Perkins, Junior. That's the way
The world was made and that's the way it will
Continue to the end, unless it's changed.
Yet Peter Perkins when his hour had struck
Lay down and died. What else was there to do?"

SONGS OF FAITH IN THE YEAR AFTER NEXT

II

I do not like to be alone:
My solar plexus turns to stone;
And yet, I know of nothing worse'n
Living with another person;
I hate to be a bachelor,
And marriage likewise, I abhor:—
Emphatically I resent
The things that people don't invent.

III

The year is at the spring, and so
Things begin to spring and grow;
Trees afford a shade, e.g.,
For those who can afford a tree;
Robins chirp and roses flourish;
Esculent herbs begin to nourish;
Fields are rife with floral data,
Which cows and sheep consume, pro rata;
Nature, squiffed on pre-war May,
Simply throws the stuff away:—
Four out of five, as things are now,
Get pyorrhea, anyhow.

IV

Grant me, O Lord, no neater rhyme,
Nor use nor usufruct of pelf,

But just a thought, from time to time,
Of something other than myself!

Oh, let me think of bug or beef;
Of Bismarck or the Caspian Sea,
Of anything to get relief
From that confounded nuisance, me!

I know myself quite well by heart;
I know the business of my soul,
And I should very gladly part
From that pestiferous rigmarole.

Oh, let me think of Joan of Arc;
Of truffles, queens and kitchen-maids;
Of George the Fifth and Central Park;
Of cheese and Labor Day parades!

Oh, let me think of Lipton's tea;
Of Prester John and Pilsen beer,
Of any bloomin' thing but me,
And that eternal, *"Weh is mir!"*

V

Soldiers have to fight and swear
To win the stripes they proudly wear;
While zebras, most unfit for war,
Have stripes enough to fill a corps.
Such unequal distribution
Is part of Heaven's constitution.

[159]

XII

The brook comes tumbling down the hill
With H_2-O the stream to fill;
The stream, it hurries all aquiver
With water for the richer river,
Which, in its turn, eternally
Runs with oblations to the sea;
But when the sea steams up in rain,
They get their water back again:—
None flies to serve another's ends
Without a thought of dividends.

XIII

The turnip and the cabbage are
Not lovely as a rose or star;
The beet and radish in the stilly
Earth, compare not with the lily;
A cow or sheep is not to be
Considered with a peony;
And yet, they brew delicious juices,
That have their sound plebeian uses;
Sans which, we'd all turn up our toes
At lily, peony or rose:—
Alas, that Beauty's thousand graces
Depend on Nature's homely phases!

XIV

The lapidary care bestowed
By God in fashioning the toad;
The expert craftsmanship which He
Spent on the gnu's topography;
The thought which loosened from that Brow
The crab, the camel and the cow,
With equal lavishness He spent
On many a priest and president.

XV

The horse, on his ferruginous feet,
Stands patient in the muggy street,
Untied, unguarded, and so free
To make a dash for liberty;
And yet, he stands and knows no goad
To shake his servitude and load,
And waits and bears the heat because
No rein is tugging at his jaws.
I watch the little men who pass
That dumb and dinosauric mass,
Whom he might, with a casual hoof,
Consign to the domain called "Pouf!"
And feel in every line and limb
Contemptuous of the likes of him.

[163]

Anthropological Note

When the mountains rose from fire,
And the seas fell down between,
Ere the rock confessed desire
In a bacchanal of green;
When Earth sizzled like a sun,
And the steaming tempest raved,
There was none to sin, and none
To be damned or to be saved.

In that time the Lord could look
From His heavenly balcony
On a land no sages shook,
On a free and fishless sea;
There was neither beast nor bird
To disturb His quiet days;
None to slay Him with a word,
None to damn Him or to praise.

INTERLUDE, FOR A SOLITARY FLUTE

Much have I felt and much have seen,
And now I know a life may break
As a twig is broken from a tree—
God pity all our company,
If God there be!

For now I know how rare a thing
Is this despair I used to sing!

Let those who can, cling close to God,
Against the day when this may be:
Ibis or priest or fane or fire,
Totem or tomb or creed or choir;

Seize Him in sky or sea or sod,
Temple or hill or scroll or tree:
There is no other song will bear
So dread a burden as despair!

Cling close to Him, forlorn Man;
Cling close to Him in bog or spire:
There is no other song will bear
So still a burden as despair!

For now I know how rare a thing
Is this despair I used to sing!

Sing it, sing it, if you can;
String for the song a lesser lyre,
And see how suddenly the note
Dies on the steel in brain and throat!

I know how rare, how rare a thing
Is this despair
I used to sing!

II

Some shall dig
The hills of Use,
And some shall follow
The Gold Wild Goose.

And the hills shall open
And be revealed,
And their glittering fruits
The rocks shall yield—

Thrones and chariots
For lords of Use,
And death for the hunters
Of the Gold Wild Goose—

The Gold Wild Goose
That cries in the mist
With the voice of Buddha,
The voice of Christ,

The voice of Mohammed,
And Moses' voice,
Till they who hear it
Rise and rejoice—

And she will bear him
This bastard twain—
The monster, Fear
And the hunchback, Pain.

A man may lie
With her, and she
Leave in his arms
The salt of the sea;

A knife in his heart,
And drouth on his breath,
Terror and Pain—
But never, Death.

But Sorrow, that cries
Like a wind on water,
Is still of Eve
A natural daughter.

For a man may lie
With her, and she
Will give herself unto him
Utterly,

Till the sun's red thunder,
The night's black drum
Cease, and his love
His peace become.

IV

We took our love by each white hand
And went into a summer land,
Where fadeless fruit and blossoms blew,
And amaranth and lotus grew.

And there the flower of sleep we ate,
And bared the breast of our dreams to fate,
And when the veins of the moon ran white,
We drank the ichor in leaves of night.

And yet we knew, we knew it well,
That love must tread the asphodel;
That noon would conquer with drums and brass
The honied silence of love and grass.

The hours that fell at our feet we threw
Like fretful pebbles into the blue,
And when the eyes of our love looked far,
We screened his dream with the morning-star.

When sundown sang of a day that's dead,
We twined the amaranth round love's head;
We laughed our thought of the singing free,
And lifted love for the sun to see.

And yet we knew, we knew it well,
That love must walk on the asphodel;
That time would conquer with steel and brass
The pitiful heaven of all who pass.

[179]

Sorrow shall not know us,
Though we be her tears;
Time shall not trouble us,
Though we be as her years;
For we shall be the silence
That sits behind the door,
In the long time coming
Evermore.

VII

No tree where lunar angels light,
No birds whose feathers are afire,
No hallelujahs in the night,
When stars and silence are the choir.

No apparitions in the dawn,
No sprite mercurial in the moon;
The vision and the music gone,
That were the first and only boon.

Only the ground with stones and worms,
Only the road that's hard and long,
Only the twisted human forms
Whose labor is their only song.

Only the hour of troubled dust,
The brambled bower, the windy ways;
And shall I say, "Come, share my crust,
Come share my cruse of stagnant days—

"My love, whose wandering eyes still sail
Like ships upon the burning west;
For whom the enchanted nightingale
Sings Latmos up within your breast"?

And shall I say, "Let Latmos be:
Endymion wanders, lost and blind,
The endless night of Thessaly
Whose nightingale is but a wind"?

My love, tall ships with chiselled prows
Still sail where Triton shields his eyes,
And silver under silver boughs,
Endymion waits the moon to rise.

My love, for you the knightly years
Stand golden in the sundown's fire;
For you the hills uncross their spears
And bid you pass to your desire.

And shall I say, "Come, pause with me,
Whose springs are weary of their seed"?
And shall I so unfaithful be
To your dear love for my drear need.

Your mantle of blue waters don;
The lands with festival are rife;
Your shoes of loveliness put on,
And go, my love, and welcome life.

X

It is not Beauty's fault that I
No longer listen or reply,
When in a thousand various tones,
She plays her drums and saxophones,
To call, with sensitive alarms,
My spirit to creative arms.

It is not Beauty's fault, I gaze
With mackerel eye upon her ways;
Her greens and seres and lights and shades,
Her bright tableaux and swift parades.

My spirit still would much endure
To be her slave and paramour;
To be a partner in her spring,
And share her winter sorrowing;
To spend her suns' unminted gold,
And race her winds through hot and cold,
Or toss the silver of her moons
On bars of her divine saloons.

Alas, her gifts no longer stir
Because my glands are through with her!

XI

With me my little world shall die,
My personal earth, peculiar sky,
My biased God and special sight
Of trees and men and day and night;—
A sudden, conscious gleam withdrawn
From that great glass which mirrors dawn:
Two tangible hands, that reach above,
To that fierce groping which is Love,
And lead him down their narrow way
To warmth and refuge for a day.

My eyes have helped bewildered spheres
A pace or two along the years,
And my reality has given
An hour of glory unto Heaven;
My thought has shot its impulses
Through ocean's mighty arteries;
And bits of disentangled mud
Have drained the scarlet of my blood;
Have stolen the quickness of my breath
To stand like roses, flaunting Death.

Oh, I have been a friend to bless
To all the host of nothingness;
Have shared my tiny store—and yet
How soon these ingrate things forget:
The earth, the sea, the rose, the sky,
They'll get themselves another guy!

I understand that women are
As fickle as a gift cigar,
And, as for all that I can say,
It may be so (I've been away)
But, fickle as the fair may be,
They're constant as calamity,
Compared to a capricious cuss
Who sports the name of Morph-e-us.

He'll say, "Lie down—I'm standing near;
Go pound (in ancient Greek) your ear;
Go linger in the poppy-dells,
And polish up your aging cells:
Your thyroid looks a trifle blue;
Your joints are drinking up the dew;
Your outlook's wild, your credit's wan,
And trucks will soon distribute dawn—
So, go and tumble in the hay;
Tomorrow is a tougher day!"

Oh, many a time (and even oft)
My billion-buttoned clothes I've doffed,
And hopeful as a babe unborn,
Prepared to sleep through dawn and horn.
I've thought of streams and forests cool,
And perfect shots in Kelly pool;
Of pastures where Pavlowa sheep
Interpret deep and dreamless sleep;

I've counted sheep and lamb and ewe,
Till we were mingled in a stew,
And in a dark and fatal hour,
My brave arithmetic went sour.
I've thought of dark and restful shades,
And not so dark or restful maids,
Of trees and cabbages in rows,
And this and that and them and those,
Till three-inch skies across the way,
Grew lovely with an eight-hour day;—
And yet, for everything I tried,
You'd think the bloody Greek had died.

Oh, go and say that women are
As changeful as a bootleg bar;
As Heaven's intent—but do not dare
Their fickleness to this compare.
Oh, do not dare, for if you do,
I fear I shall agree with you.

CAROL FOR THE DAY AFTER CHRISTMAS

Carol for the Day After Christmas

I burn a reverential rhyme
Unto the modest Muse of Crime,
Unsung, unhung (I mean with bays)
But generous to her devotees;—

Not indiscriminately kind;
No friend to the burglarious mind;
No dour divinity of jail—
But Crime on an Extensive Scale!

Dear Muse (for nobler numbers fit)
Of Those Who Get Away With It;
For whom the fiscal welkin rings
With praise of cabinets and kings;

In whose benign and fecund shade
The grapevine sacrifice is made
By Forward-Looking Men, who know
Your cabalistic So-and-So;

*Love-songs, at Once Tender and Informative
—An Unusual Combination in Verses of This
Character*

I

Satyrs used to fall for nymphs,
Just the same as other symphs;
Same as many a modern goof,
Cupid kept them on the hoof.

II

A woman, like the touted Sphinx,
Sits, and God knows what she thinks;
Hard-boiled men, who never fall,
Say she doesn't think at all.

Your little soul,
Your little mind!

XIV

Love, you brought me everything;
I gave little—
But the beauty that I sing
May be brittle;—

May be brittle, and so might—
Now I've spoken!—
Have fallen on another's sight
And been broken!

XV

The honey of the Hybla bees
Is not so sweet as kissing you;
Nor autumn wind in dying trees
So wistful is as missing you.

And when you are not mine to kiss,
My every thought is haunting you;
And when your mouth is mine, I miss
The wistfulness of wanting you.

XVI

Here we are together,
You and I,
In the amber autumn weather,
Yet we sigh,
And are quiet, disenchanted
By the bliss
That convinced us that we wanted
Only this!

Yet is this a cause for weeping
After all?
Isn't this a time for keeping
Festival,
When the high gods make decision
And ordain
That poor Cupid have his vision
Back again?

XVII

The lady of my heart is one
Who has no peer beneath the sun;
But mortal truths have mortal sequels—
Beneath the moon I know her equals.

[211]

In those serene and potent eyes
Is there no kindly compromise?
Will they not grant me this release:
To see their light and still have peace,
And let the deeps behind them be
For sturdier fish the fatal sea?

EPILOGUE